T0182608

A Coyote's Tale

THIS EDITION

Editorial Management by Oriel Square
Produced for DK by WonderLab Group LLC
Jennifer Emmett, Erica Green, Kate Hale, *Founders*

Editor Maya Myers; **Photography Editor** Nicole DiMella; **Managing Editor** Rachel Houghton;
Designers Project Design Company; **Researcher** Michelle Harris;
Copy Editor Lori Merritt; **Indexer** Connie Binder; **Proofreader** Susan K. Hom;
Authenticity Reader Dr. Naomi R. Caldwell; **Series Reading Specialist** Dr. Jennifer Albro

First American Edition, 2024
Published in the United States by DK Publishing, a division of Penguin Random House LLC
1745 Broadway, 20th Floor, New York, NY 10019

Copyright © 2024 Dorling Kindersley Limited
24 25 26 27 10 9 8 7 6 5 4 3 2 1
001-339789-Sep/2024

A catalog record for this book is available from the Library of Congress.
HC ISBN: 978-0-7440-9446-6
PB ISBN: 978-0-7440-9445-9

DK books are available at special discounts when purchased in bulk for sales promotions, premiums, fund-raising,
or educational use. For details, contact:
DK Publishing Special Markets, 1745 Broadway, 20th Floor, New York, NY 10019
SpecialSales@dk.com

Printed and bound in China

The publisher would like to thank the following for their kind permission to reproduce their images:
a=above; c=center; b=below; l=left; r=right; t=top; b/g=background
Alamy Stock Photo: Don Geyer 5bc, Suzi Eszterhas / Minden Pictures 6-7, Ernst Mutchnick 4bc, 23tl;
Depositphotos Inc: jill@ghostbear.org 3; **Dreamstime.com:** Rinus Baak 21bc, Jim Cumming 17br,
Donyanedomam 12bc, 13br, Moose Henderson 11br, Chris Hill 9bl, Mary Hynes 22, Muriel Lasure 8-9,
Mikael Males 13bl, 19br, Pimmimemom 10-11, Rixie 15bc, Tartilastock 18crb (background), Wisconsinart 18bc;
Getty Images: Stu Smith / 500px 18-19, Gallo Images ROOTS RF collection / Danita Delimont 6bc, 23bl,
Moment / David C Stephens 16-17, 21crb, 23clb; **Getty Images / iStock:** E+ / KeithSzafranski 5br, 6br,
kojihirano 10bc, Eloi_Omella 14-15, Terje71 20-21, vodoleyka 14bc; **Danielle V. Green:** 20bc;
naturepl.com: Sebastian Kennerknecht 16bc, George Sanker 7br; **Shutterstock.com:** J Curtis 8bc, 9br,
marmarto 18crb, Warren Metcalf 4-5, 12-13, 23cla, 23cl, OlgaChernyak 1, 15br

Cover images: *Front:* **Dreamstime.com:** Nataliia Darmoroz, Anna Lopatina br;
Shutterstock.com: AZ 54design clb; *Back:* **Dreamstime.com:** Az Septian cra

All other images © Dorling Kindersley Limited
For more information see: www.dkimages.com

www.dk.com

MIX
Paper | Supporting
responsible forestry
FSC™ C018179

This book was made with Forest
Stewardship Council™ certified
paper – one small step in DK's
commitment to a sustainable future.
Learn more at
www.dk.com/uk/information/sustainability

A Coyote's Tale

Angela Modany

It is spring in
the desert.
The desert is a
coyote's home.
The coyote looks
for a den.
It will have babies
in the den.

den

The coyote
babies are born.
They are called pups.
The pups drink their
mother's milk.
Their eyes are closed.
They cannot see yet.

pup

rabbit

It is summer.
The pups leave the den.
They grow bigger.
The pups learn to hunt.
They hunt rabbits
and squirrels.

The coyote smells other animals with its nose.
The coyote is fast.
It chases the animals.

nose

The coyote howls.
This tells other coyotes
where it is.
It barks when it
sees a wolf.
The bark tells
other coyotes
about the wolf.
This helps the
coyotes stay safe.

wolf

People live near
the coyote.
They hear the coyote.
They believe the coyote
put the stars in the sky.

stars

pack

The coyote meets
other coyotes.
They form a pack.
The pack hunts
together.

The weather
gets colder.
It is winter.
People tell stories
about the coyote.
They only tell these
stories in the winter.
They tell the stories
out loud.

winter

The stories tell how the coyote is smart. The coyote plays tricks in the stories. Children learn from the coyote.

tricks

Spring comes again.
The people stop telling
stories about the coyote.
The coyote goes
back to its den.
Soon, there will be
new coyote pups.

Glossary

den
a wild animal's home

desert
a dry habitat that has few
plants and gets little rain

howl
to make a long, loud noise
that sounds like a dog

pack
a group of the same
kind of animal

pup
a baby coyote

Quiz

Answer the questions to see what you have learned. Check your answers with an adult.

1. What are coyote babies called?

2. Where do coyotes have their babies?

3. What sounds does a coyote make?

4. When do people tell stories about the coyote?

5. What is a group of coyotes called?

1. Pups 2. A den 3. Howls and barks 4. Winter 5. A pack